LOGOS

ESSENTIAL POETS SERIES 229

LOGOS

GIL FAGIANI

GUERNICA
TORONTO – BUFFALO – LANCASTER (U.K.)
2015

Michael Mirolla, general editor
Guernica Editions Inc.
1569 Heritage Way, Oakville, (ON), Canada L6M 2Z7
2250 Military Road, Tonawanda, N.Y. 14150-6000 U.S.A.

Proofreading: "100 Proof"
Book design by Jamie Kerry of Belle Étoile Studios

Distributors:
University of Toronto Press Distribution,
5201 Dufferin Street, Toronto (ON), Canada M3H 5T8
Gazelle Book Services, White Cross Mills, High
Town, Lancaster LA1 4XS U.K.

First edition.
Printed in Canada.

Legal Deposit – First Quarter
Library of Congress Catalog Card Number: 2014950177
Library and Archives Canada Cataloguing in Publication

Fagiani, Gil, author
Logos / Gil Fagiani. -- 1st edition.

(Essential poets series ; 229)
Poems.
Issued in print and electronic formats.
ISBN 978-1-77183-017-1 (pbk.).--
ISBN 978-1-77183-018-8 (epub).--
ISBN 978-1-77183-019-5 (mobi)
I. Title. II. Series: Essential poets series ; 229
PS3606.A42L64 2015   811'.6   C2014-906214-1
                                    C2014-906215-X

*I dedicate this book to Lou Zinzi,
Carmen Rodriguez, and all those who
passed through the doors of Logos, 1969-73.*

Contents

SHOOTING DOPE WITH TROTSKY

WHITE UNCLE TOM

SIDING WITH THE ENEMY

A SINGLE SPARK

INTRODUCTION

When I told my mother in 1968 – a few weeks before my 23rd birthday – that I had a heroin problem, she wept in despair. She grew up in New York City's West Village and knew heroin addicts. And what she knew about them was that, except for imprisonment or death, they could never stop using. With the broad range of treatment options available for substance abusers today, it's easy to forget that heroin addiction was once considered a hopeless condition, and the popular belief "once a dopefiend, always a dopefiend" remained unchallenged until the 1960s.

During that period, heroin use spread from mostly poor Black and Latino neighborhoods to white, middle-class communities and, in response, there emerged a proliferation of residential treatment programs called *therapeutic communities* (TCs). Their initial inspiration was Synanon, founded in 1958 by Chuck Dederich in Santa Monica, California. He created a drug-free community that incorporated the basic Alcoholics Anonymous model of using recovering addicts as co-therapists in a peer-based environment. Key to this approach were encounter sessions known as "The Game," which consisted of confrontational techniques designed to strip down a person's defense mechanisms to uncover the real person.

Early TCs were leery of the mental-health establishment, and viewed professionals as ignorant bunglers, at best, and enablers, at worst. TCs had their defects: there was little oversight of staff, who sometimes had Napoleon complexes; training was limited; psychiatric and cognitive disorders went untreated; and some program sanctions, like shaving heads, violated a resident's dignity.

Back then, TCs underestimated the danger alcohol use posed to a heroin addict's recovery and permitted senior residents to drink in moderation. As a result, many people whose TC experience made it possible for them to never use heroin again – and I include myself in this group – became alcoholics later in life.

The pluses in the old-school TC outweighed the shortfalls. With a minimum of paperwork and administrative requirements, the staff spent more time with residents, participating in both therapeutic and cultural activities. TCs were more flexible and experimental, encouraging innovative techniques such as Gestalt therapy, memoir writing, drama, and psychodrama. Above all, the dogma of heroin's invincibility was discredited.

As for me, I view my 14 months, from November 1969 to January 1971, in Logos, a South Bronx-based TC, as nothing less than lifesaving. Aside from my physical survival, Logos helped me gain crucial insights into myself and my family, develop a capacity for leadership, and perhaps most importantly, I acquired an emotional toughness that for 40 years has served me well in coping with family and work crises.

I took advantage of my stay at Logos to read extensively and to indulge my fascination for language by jotting down slang and idioms. I began to do this years earlier while still a cadet at Pennsylvania Military College, when I spent the summer of 1966 in Spanish Harlem as part of a Cornell student project, and was struck with how expressive and imaginative neighborhood people's language could be.

This poetry of the people, this song of the streets, has been the most influential element in my literary pursuits, and why my first impulse is to write about the world of addiction and treatment by means of poetry rather than prose.

My stay at Logos coincided with a period of tumultuous social and political unrest. In the background was the Civil Rights Movement, the protests against the Vietnam War, and Women's and Gay Liberation. Fed up with a tyrannical director, the lack of a re-entry phase to the program, including employment opportunities, and talk of transforming Logos into a utopian community, most of the senior residents rebelled against the staff in February 1971.

Leaving Logos en masse, we formed the Spirit of Logos (SOL), and initially sought governmental recognition and funding. When this strategy failed, the SOL dissolved. I was among a group who founded a radical organization called White Lightning that allied with revolutionary groups such as the Black Panthers and the Young Lords, focusing on the political and economic dimensions of drug addiction.

I am particularly grateful to my cousin, Don Cavellini, and legendary TC administrator Carlos Pagán, for steering me towards Logos, and Lou Zinzi, the director of Logos I, who died several months after I entered the program. His charismatic example aroused within me the desire and commitment to change.

Finally, my Logos experiences – both good and bad – helped guide me in the 21 years that I directed Renewal House, a modified therapeutic community affiliated with Project Renewal, located in Downtown Brooklyn.

For readers unfamiliar with drug argot, TC jargon, and particular historical references, I have provided a glossary at the end of the book.

– *Gil Fagiani*

*Just 'cause you got the monkey off your back
doesn't mean the circus left town.*

– George Carlin

Believer

On a muggy
fly-filled day
inside a courtyard
reeking of diapers,
mice-filled glue traps,
take-out tins of rice and beans,
he stands behind a long line
of sick junkies
until it's his turn
to push his last ten-dollar bill
through a hole in the wall,
convinced
a dynamite sack of dope
is going to be pushed back.

SHOOTING DOPE
WITH TROTSKY

Gray Zone

Pennsylvania Military College, 1964

I fidget in the shadows
of a fleabag hotel
feeling incandescent
in my cadet grays,
waiting for Ted and Joe-Joe
who are upstairs
with two prostitutes.
I hadn't the heart to join them
though we vowed to be
all for one and one for all
on the manly mission of whoring.

We're in a Black section of town,
half-blind on Old Grand-Dad,
the hookers with prizefighter faces.
I hear Joe-Joe, *What the fuck?*
furniture crashing, muffled groans.
Joe-Joe stomps down the stairs.
She has a shlong twice the size of mine!
Ted follows, rubbing his knuckles.

Outside, prostitutes
with platinum wigs
and celery-stalk teeth.
Hey, Generals, one of them says,
where y'all goin'?

Changing Stripes

We love pumping iron,
Craig, senior private, six foot two,
former football player
and I, junior private,
two heads shorter than him
but bench-pressing double my bodyweight.

We're workout buddies
spot each other
when we put on fifty pound plates,
tearing down the shower bars,
doing chin-ups in the latrine
admire each other's biceps and triceps.

The summer of '66,
I volunteer with my cousin
in an anti-poverty program in Harlem,
protest against slumlords,
brutal cops, the Vietnam War,
return to the Cadet Corps
concerned about bigger issues
than bodybuilding.

I fight with classmates
over free speech, law and order,
the draft, brand them
brain-dead, bigots, saber-rattlers.
Instead of martial music,
I march to the beat of Bob Dylan,
Joan Baez, Ray Barretto.

One day a heavy fist falls on my door.
It's Craig. *Just want to see,*
with my own eyes, he says,
scoping out my arms and chest,
how much you let yourself go.
I ball my fists to hide
the marijuana stains on my fingers.

Sisters

The college mixer was a bust and the Gallo Port that Ted and I downed left us feeling more drowsy than drunk. We were heading for the exit when we ran into two Black women walking down the hallway, cackling and cracking gum. I smiled and Ted sang out *Soul!* and snapped his fingers. After a friendly exchange, the women – who were sisters – invited us to a party, and soon we were in the boonies of South Jersey, trailing behind them in Ted's 1952 Mercedes Benz convertible, which his father had just given him as a birthday gift. Ted didn't know how to use a manual transmission, and had been stalling the engine out all day. Just before we left, one of the sisters introduced me to a Black guy in the parking lot, and later I thought how he had seemed to freeze up when I reached over to shake his hand. After a half-hour drive, a car with glaring headlights shot past us, cutting us off a hundred yards ahead. We ended up on the side of the road to avoid a collision. Through the darkness, we saw Black men scrambling towards us with bats and tire irons. Ted fumbled with the gear shift, stalling the engine out, then restarted it, only to have the wheels spin wildly on the soft shoulder. With our attackers only a few feet away, the wheels finally gripped something solid, and we skidded on to the road. As we sped towards Philadelphia, I fiddled with the radio, trying to find some music, but except for a brief blast of a minister's sermon, all we heard was static.

Countdown

I quit shaving my upper lip.
The cadet officers don't care;
it's the regular Army officers
I have to watch out for.
Whenever I see one coming
I pull out a handkerchief
and fake like I'm sneezing.

Unlike other seniors,
who set their sights on vacation,
career, graduate school, 'Nam,
I'm moving to Spanish Harlem
working with a tenants' group,
need a moustache to blend
into the neighborhood.

Early one morning
my door swings open
a flashlight finds my face.
Commandant Colonel Mazer
marches me off to the latrine,
orders me to shear off my 'stache.

The Commandant says
he'd give me the boot
but only two weeks remain
of my cadet career.
So until the final day
I have to report to his orderly
pre-reveille, face smooth as a bullet.

Utopia

Spanish Harlem, 1967

No bosses, teachers, lames
Studs take me under their wing
School me in the fine points of hip talk

Home is 104th, between Park and Lex
Las chicas son muy preciosas
From the shingaling to the mambo

La Marketa is a museum of food, fabric, spices
Stroll in Central Park, swim in Jefferson Pool
Snow cone and hot dog carts line Third Avenue

Thrill to the chill of blackberry wine
Cops speed by, keep their distance
Yerba is top-shelf and everywhere

Dump my palooka past for tropical
Currents in an ocean of laughter

Hollywood

I lay up in my cousin's pad,
getting lessons on being hip
from DJ Frankie
"Hollywood" Crocker,
who promises to put
more pep in my step,
more dip in my hip.

I see junkies sprawled
on the sidewalk below,
convince myself –
Connecticut-bred
and Hollywood hip-notized –
I can dabble in dope
without getting strung out.

First time, I take two toots
in each nostril,
lose my fear, end up making it
with my jailed friend's wife.
In my head I hear one
of Hollywood's foxettes
gush, *Do it Frankie, do it to it!*

The second time, I skin-pop,
almost OD, body mush,
vomiting in the street.
Neighbors squeal to my cousin.

I swear I was drunk.
The locals know
dope from booze.

I lay off the H,
stick to wine and weed,
counting on Hollywood's
music and patter to put
more glide in my stride,
close the hole in my soul.

Just Out of Jail

Hungry for a high, I run into Héctor on 105th Street. *¿Estás en algo? – Are you into something?* I ask. *I gotta be cool*, he drawls. *I just got out of jail.* I hand him a sawbuck and he disappears into a building across the street. Twenty minutes go by and I start worrying that he bought the dope and booked out a back door, beating the *blanquito –* the white boy. I cross the street to peep the scene, when a polar bear in a flannel shirt pulls me into the pissy hallway and pats me down. *If I find a spike, I'll break your back.* Inside, Héctor has his feet spread and his hands against a wall. A pitted face snarls: *Take it all off!* Shirt, pants, underwear, shoes pile up on the floor. A *viejita –* old lady – clomps down the stairs in her bathrobe and slippers. She sees Héctor's shiny brown ass. *Adiós mio!* she cries, clomping back up the stairs. *See*, Héctor says, *I told you I don't have anything.* The narco is about to leave when he fingers Héctor's Marlboro pack and fishes out a deck of heroin. *Scram!* he says to me. *And stay away from spics!* On my way out, I watch as he stuffs Héctor in the back seat of a green Plymouth. In the rear window, I see the blur of blackjacks, as Héctor crouches in a corner and tries to dodge the blows.

Speed (Sean)

When a three-day bender
costs me my bank clerk's job,
my mother makes the sign of the cross
and calls me Good-Time Charlie.
I'm her last-born and she dotes on me,
so I laugh, wave her words away
tell her not to worry
I'll lay off the lush
and find another nine-to-five.

But work's a grind.
I'm into fun, high times
and, along with Nicky De Vito,
start messing with crystal meth.
Our veins hum like high-voltage wires
moonlight melts into sunshine,
motion becomes our devotion.

At home I clean the upstairs crapper
twenty times,
the bowl blazing
the pine soap and ammonia scalding my lungs.
My mother says *enough already*
and swats me with a toilet brush
after I scrub out the grout between the floor tile.

At his house, Nicky sits by a basement workbench
polishing a new pair of shoes
until he wears through the soles,

breaks off heels,
hiding the ruined footware from his father,
who dishes out bare-knuckled discipline.

Once at Nicky's place,
we mainline two hype sticks of meth,
guzzle all the guinea booze in the liquor cabinet:
Strega, Campari, Frangelico, Anisette, Grappa.
Nicky flips on the new Motorola TV
complains about snowy reception
and begins taking the TV apart,
swearing he can fix and reassemble it
before his folks return home.

We spread all the screws, springs,
wires, tubes, and knobs across the carpet floor,
the first thing his parents see
when they open the front door.

Bricklayer by profession,
his father can haul a hod of cement
like it's a foam cushion.
He flattens Nicky with one blow,
knocking over a lamp,
killing the light.

I rush the front door,
weave between cars
until I reach my house,
my ticker feeling like it's going
to tear through my rib cage,
my mother throwing holy water on me
as I run up the stairs.

Oil Burner (Georgie)

I'm behind bars
kicking the worst dope habit of my life
– a real oil burner – the old-timers say.
In the streets I swap my beer-cap cooker
for a gallon jug top to cook the half load
I pump in my arm just to take the edges off.
The second day I barf and crap at the same time.
Luckily, the sink and toilet are next to each other,
so I don't drown in a swamp of puke and diarrhea.

The third day a screw comes and says,
to get methadone for my withdrawal pains,
I have to sign a form and commit myself
to the Rockefeller Program.
I say, *I'll sign anything, just get me some meth.*
I'll be back, the screw says.
For ten days I thrash in bed,
muscles feeling like they're being ripped off my bones,
body fluids reek, can't catch a wink of sleep.
The greatest torture is marching into the mess hall;
the smell of chipped beef, stewed tomatoes,
and banana pudding makes my guts flip.

Day thirteen, the screw comes back,
takes me to the clinic.
I tell him to take his form
and five-year commitment to the Rockefeller Program
and shove it up his shit chute.
In less than a week I'm out on the street again,
learned my lesson well.
From now on, I'll keep my fix down
to what fits in a beer-cap cooker.

My Bag, His Bag (Seth)

Dad's a doctor, and I shoot up anything I can swipe from his black bag. Sometimes it's muscle relaxant, and I schlep around like my body's been wrung out of a clothes dryer. Other times it's heart stimulant, and my eyes bulge like the bottoms of shot glasses. Still others, it's psych meds, making my mouth foam, and my arms twitchy as dandelions in a wind storm. Every so often I luck out and find Blue Beauties – morphine tablets – I pulverize and inject lovingly into a vein, singing, *Everybody's beautiful* ... kissing my mom, my brother, the neighbors' kids, the mailman, the newspaper boy, stray dogs, TV screens, political posters, bus ads. Usually when I clip his bag, dad acts like he doesn't notice, even if I'm crawling on the floor. But after a few of my Blue Beauty lovefests, he commits me to an out-of-state rehab.

Treatment

Through the fog banks
of Kools, Marlboros,
Chiva-Chiva, Sinsemilla,
pussy incense, Thai sticks,
I see his scalped head,
pink like a Spalding,
with nicks and blood traces
of a dull razor.

What's with Frenchie's noggin?
I ask Chino,
as I tear the top off
another two-dollar bag
of Cabeza's dyno dugee
and glare at Chino
as he holds a folded match
cover, ready to dig in.

He was in Phoenix House
and they shaved his head
for mouthing off to a counselor.

I watch Frenchie's eyes close —
a shadow covers
his face,
his Spalding
bobbing inches away from
the table's edge.

What a pendejo,
Chino says, in between snorts.

He should have split the program
before they turned his head
into a coco pelao — a skinned coconut.

Democratic Convention, 1968

I snort all my stash
in the bus bathroom
on my way to Chicago
to protest the war in Vietnam
with my girlfriend Nilsa.

In the Windy City,
Mayor Daley bans
public rallies, marches,
orders the National Guard
to shoot to kill and maim.

At the hostel
where we stay,
flowers are passed out
to put in the soldiers'
rifle barrels.

In Lincoln Park:
someone shouts
Liberate the truck!
and a hundred hands
steal everything edible.

Beery-breath cops
clear Grant Park
with searchlights
mounted on street cleaners
fogging tear gas.

Crashing barricades,
we charge through Old Town,
blocking traffic,
breaking windows,
pillaging souvenir shops.

I ditch Nilsa
at an MC-5 concert,
desperate for a dope dealer
to keep me from having
to kick cold turkey.

Mobbed by bodyguards
Bobby Seale shouts:
We gotta barbecue some pork!
Dillinger: *Militant nonviolence!*
Ginsberg intones, *Om!*

Marching with Flower Cong
I suck down
a half pint of Wilson's,
withering from waves
of pain and nausea.

On Michigan Avenue,
police chant: *Kill! Kill!*
beat protesters, reporters,
bystanders, shove them
through plate-glass windows.

Camera crews
dodge lead-lined gloves,
mace, rocks, gas canisters.
Thousands roar:
The Whole World Is Watching!

On the return ride,
I retch my guts
into a steel can,
dreaming of peace
in a wine-cap cooker.

Shooting Dope with Trotsky

I score some hefty bags of scag
from Old Man Cano on East 118th Street
the *viejito* – 40-plus years in the dope game –
who once ODed on Christmas Eve
and leaned into a radiator,
leaving a burn scar down the middle of his head.

I rush to the East Village
and buy a mess of Trotskyist newspapers:
Vanguard, Fighting Worker, Theory and Practice,
march into a NYU bathroom,
lock myself up in a vast marble stall
and shoot Cano's sacks into my arm.

After reading competing accounts
of the 1921 Kronstadt Rebellion,
the Minneapolis Teamster Strike of 1934,
I nod off to the lullaby
of *The ABC of Materialist Dialectics,*
the negation, of the negation, of the negation.

Woodstock

Waving a long, brown finger in my face, Nilsa warned me early in the week not to do anything stupid and spoil the upcoming weekend. By "stupid," she meant getting high on dope, which, except for a snort here and there, I'd stayed away from since I signed myself out of a mental hospital in Connecticut in June after a two-week detox.

I could dig where Nilsa was coming from, but I was damned if I was going to Woodstock and hear Sly and the Family Stone sing "I Wanna Take You Higher" and Grace Slick shout *Feed your head!* without having something righteous for my own head. Of course, I swore I'd be discreet, and most definitely maintain my cool when I was with my lady. Even though we hadn't been together long, I was planning on settling down and living with her. In my book, the only thing less than *perfecto* about Nilsa was her Latin temper, which at times led her to carry on to the point of taking a swing at me.

Starting on Wednesday, rumors lit up the doper's hotline that two people had ODed after scoring from Italians on 115th Street. It stood to reason they would have something super-potent since they wholesaled heroin for all of Harlem. I hung out with Blacks and Puerto Ricans, and stayed out of Vinnie-Ville, as my friends called the Pleasant Avenue neighborhood. Besides, those Italians were a bunch of crazies, ready to break your legs for the smallest beef.

But a voice taunted me. Why not get one last hellified jolt? It would be my swan song. I wouldn't get greedy. The first and last time I'd cop from Italians and then bye-bye dope forever.

On Friday morning, I hit 115th and my guts tightened like they always did whenever I was about to score. The building I had to cop from was across from Our Lady of Mount Carmel Church, in the heart of the old Italian neighborhood. The dealer had a pitted face and a nozzle-like nose that seemed to start from the center of his forehead. I couldn't look him directly in the face. We carried out our business in silence. I gave him six bucks, flashed three fingers, and he handed me three deuce bags.

At first, I thought about sniffing a bag and saving the rest for the Woodstock Festival. But then I figured, why not get blasted now and mellow down for the weekend; this way, Nilsa would be calmer and learn to trust me. In the end, I decided to mainline a couple of bags, and went to my old hangout on 104th Street to borrow a set of gimmicks – the spike and cooker – to shoot up. The first person I saw on the block was Donna, one of the kids I took care of when I ran a day camp on the street two summers ago. I waved at her, and she smiled bashfully, bringing her hand up to her mouth to hide her new braces.

Next I ran into *Jíbaro,* a pimply parasite that never had a dime and wouldn't speak a word of English, but was always ready to rent out his gimmicks. I promised him a taste and we ducked into a burnt-out building, where all the floors had collapsed, and climbed a wobbly staircase to reach the rooftop. I stepped lightly because the floor was covered with window glass.

I cooked up two bags, and drew most of the dope in the first shot. As soon as the spike went into my arm, I knew I was going under. Hitting the floor, my bottom teeth sheared through my lip, and I flopped around like a fish on the glass shards. *Jíbaro* stepped over me, pulled the spike out of my arm, shot up, and split. Later, two old-timers took pity on me, slung my limp body over their shoulders and carried me down to the street.

I was covered with blood from dozens of cuts and couldn't move my legs. I managed to open one eye enough to see Donna and her mother sitting on a stoop as I stumbled past them, their eyes teary.

The two good-hearted dopefiends dragged me to a hospital on 123rd Street, where a Jamaican nurse cleaned my cuts and gave me cotton wadding soaked in something that, when pressed to my nose, kept me from passing out. Then she whacked me on the ass and told me to get lost.

Nilsa wasn't home from work a hot second before one of the local gossips – *bochincheras* –telephoned and blabbed how I'd ODed and was in no shape to go upstate. Since I'd lost my apartment, I was staying with my friend, Bruno, a half-Black, half-German transvestite who lived in a basement apartment on 118th Street.

When Nilsa came by, I was covered with bandages and barely able to raise my head. The TV was on and the announcer said the New York State Thruway was closed down, and the governor threatened to order 10,000 National Guard troops to pull the plug on the festival. I mumbled we couldn't have gone there anyway, but Nilsa's Latin temper got the best of her and she ripped up the

Woodstock tickets and threw the pieces in my face. After she left, I cursed myself for having anything to do with those Vinnie-Ville dope dealers and, later, sniffed my last deuce to round off the ragged edges.

Withdrawal

I'm chipping – using a bag
or two a day. I want to quit
but can't get it together,
in East Harlem.

Beg my parents to bankroll me
one more semester
at Pennsylvania Military College,
where I spent four years as a cadet.

I'll go as a civilian, I just need
a few more credits to cop
a diploma, then I'll get a job,
make a career in Social Work.

Mom says I'm skinny, my eyes
don't look right, why am I wearing
shiny pants like the colored people.
Are you on drugs? she blurts out.

I get huffy. *How dare you accuse
your son of such a thing!
I'm just between jobs, need
a little help finishing school.*

My father mumbles something about
this being the last goddamn time.
I say yes, of course, hope my student
deferment will save me from 'Nam.

On campus, I shoot my last bag,
bumble my way through registration,
go past cadets who seem like
gray zombies from a past life.

I swipe a few books, try to study
can't hack the jagged glass
in my joints, the lack of sleep,
my odor of rot and failure.

A pothead known as Lunatic
offers to bring me to the infirmary
but backs off, fearing he'll be
suspected of being my dealer.

I've known the nurse for years,
she's from the same seacoast town
in Sicily as my mother, she once
served espresso when I had the flu.

When it sinks in that I'm a junkie,
tears streak her face, they streak mine too
– she's almost an aunt –
then I beg her for Librium, Seconals.

Finals, 1968

The day of finals
I smoke a joint with Lunatic
who swears pot
supercharges your brain cells.

Words on the test melt into each other.
I can't get the opening drumbeat
of "Louie, Louie," by the Kingsmen,
out of my head.

The professor sits in back,
marking tests; I stare off into space.
I'm the second person
to hand in their exam and leave.

In the dorm I think about tying
a 50-pound barbell plate to my leg
and dropping myself
into the Delaware River.
I need to score something hard
and ride with Lunatic to New York.

Reaching 12th Street, by Strand,
I jump out with a suitcase of books,
tell Lunatic I'll give him gas money
on Sunday, notice a squashed pigeon
on a sewer grating.

After I sell the books,
I take the subway to 110th Street,
buy a bundle of deuce bags

from a guy stirring a fire inside
an oil barrel with a golf club.

At Frenchie's I open a bag,
realize it's only baking soda.
I hide a butcher's knife under my jacket
and head downtown, where I find the dealer,
standing with two guys in front
of the flaming barrel.

I tell him his product is garbage,
fondling the handle of my knife.
He says *bullshit*, tears open a bag,
scoops up powder with a folded match cover,
passes it to one of the guys
who takes two blows
and declares it *some dyno shit.*
I buy five more deuces,
go back to Frenchie's,
discover more baking soda.

Next morning I sell the beat dope
to my ex-girlfriend Sheryl,
buy a quart of Mister Twister,
hitchhike back to school, wake up
under the steps of the football stadium.

Kicking in Cuba

It's winter, 1969.
I'm in NYU's Loeb Auditorium
straining to hear a former economics adviser
to the Cuban Government:
strata, Russification,
primitive capital accumulation.

I'm getting sick,
the effects of the dope I snorted earlier
wearing thin.
But I'm trying to stay upbeat,
psyche myself up
for the 10th anniversary
of the Cuban Revolution.

I stare at the giant photos
of Fidel, Camilo, Che draped on the walls.
For a moment I feel fortified,
the people's forces are winning worldwide
in Cuba, Vietnam, Africa.
I tell myself I can win too.
I just need to stay away from East Harlem
and wean myself off the white powder.

I've just been accepted as a member
of the Venceremos Brigade,
and along with other supporters,
plan to spend a month in Cuba,
shoulder to shoulder with the *guajiros*
cutting sugar cane.

My eyes close as my body trembles
under my thin golf jacket.
I wonder how it's going to be kicking
in the hot tropical sun.
I don't want to burden the Cuban people
with my dope-sick body.

A side door bursts open.
A young woman wearing a black beret
– for a second I think of Tania,
Che's *compañera* in the Bolivian jungle –
screams: *"¡Escoria comunista!* – Communist scum! –
¡Abajo con el dictador Fidel!
¡Qué viva la gente cubana!"

She throws a smoky canister
that bounces on the stage, inches from the speaker.
People scream, dive for the floor.
The stage fills with acrid fumes,
but the speaker never lifts his head,
droning on, *conjunctural and structural
crises, rectification campaign.*

The force of the crowd drives me
through an exit door
the streetlights burn my eyes,
the cold wind, like a machete,
hacks through my golf jacket.

Female Troubles

I'm holed up with my folks
in Stamford, Connecticut,
taking a break from the street heat.
To keep Nilsa quiet, I enroll
in an outpatient drug program
called Renaissance in Westport,
home of Paul Newman – *the prettiest man
alive*, Mom says. I meet an ex-doper
named Bobby Olson, who gives me
a lift to the program.

The clients are *blanquitos* – white
bread – who look like daddy bankrolls
their Budweiser or wine-cooler habits.
I want to puke in their faces,
and sneak off and cop in El Barrio,
all along telling mom and my old lady
I'm making progress in the program.

Once I took a few hits before going
with Bobby, and griped how I can't stand
being around a bunch of loaded-up-the-ass
dames, and Bobby turns around, says,
*They're the best friends you'll ever have
and, by the way, did you take anything
before I picked you up?*
No way, man ... swear to God.

At the program, everyone
is on to me being buzzed-up,
and in group, a blonde pothead,

accuses me of being doped-up, and when
I swear to God, she shrieks, *You cunt!*
You're a cunt – a cunt! I'm struck dumb,
and swear I'll never take any more shit
from rich, pale-faced bitches.

Then Nilsa suspects
I'm dipping and dabbing,
telephones the Renaissance staff,
who report I haven't been seen in weeks,
tells my mom, and now I have
two more bitches on my back.

Houston, Texas, 1964 (The Great Him)

Today is the first day of the rest of your life
– Charles "Chuck" Dederich

I dig out bottles from trash cans,
pour the whiskey dregs of Old Crow,
the ghetto wine of Cool Breeze,
the piss-foam of Angel Tequila,
into a quart-sized milk jug,
sip the gasoline-hued brew
on a bus chartered by the Rotary Club
to banish the junkies
of Glen Cove, Long Island,
by consigning us to Synanon,
a beachside compound in California
run by an ex-lush who trains dopers
to use peer pressure and attack-therapy
to stay off the stuff.

Getting Help

Nilsa says it's over,
and I can only win her back
if I go into a drug program.

I put my head down, slink away.
I have less than a dollar to my name,
so I can't score any dope.

Besides, I'm steeling myself
to never use narcotics again.
At the liquor store on 112th Street,

I order a chilled pint of Thunderbird,
but as I take out three quarters, somebody
slaps the coins out of my hand.

I turn around. Behind me stands Nilsa;
she's followed me. *Go ahead –
pick up the money, you pathetic junkie.*

I stand stunned, then take off,
jump the turnstile at 110th Street,
head to the Bronx to see my cousin,

who promised he'd help get me
into Phoenix House. Now I'm
pissed I didn't pick up the quarters.

WHITE UNCLE TOM

The Interview (Sean)

After the usual questions
about commitment to change,

openness to treatment,
willingness to follow rules and regulations,

the counselor stares at Sean.
You're in the South Bronx;

*how do you know we won't cut
your throat after you fall asleep?*

How do you know I won't cut yours?
Sean stares back.

Five minutes later
he's welcomed into the program.

Drawing the Line (Sean)

Two o'clock in the morning.
I'm startled out of my sleep
by the banging of pots and pans.
Let's go! Out of bed! I'm herded
with the rest of the residents
into the community room.
Thunder crackles outside.

Program's new, poorly staffed.
I'd been taking Mom's soda money
and giving it to Julio, who's scoring
plump deuce bags on St. Ann's Avenue.
The little silver camera I bought
in Vietnam is missing, and somebody
just broke into the counselor's office
and pinched the petty cash.

Louie, the facility director,
is standing with a paintbrush,
there's a white line across the floor.
Across from him is a stool, and Julio,
with a bald head, holding a barber's shears.

This side's for the living, Louie
shouts; *the other is for the dead.*
Those who want to stay,
get your head shaved.
The rest, take a hike.

Another clap of thunder,
the wind slaps the rain

against the windows.
My family's sick of my bullshit.

With a scalped head,
I'll look like I had psycho-surgery.
Two people leave.
My locks hit the floor.

Good Times, Bad Times (Georgie)

I worked as a bagger
for Big Mikie Rodriguez.
I'd bank $3K a week.
Rode on the back of a Harley,
entered basement apartments
in row houses in the heart
of the old Italian neighborhood.
Did business with young hoods,
knit shirts, alligator kicks –
stereotypes all the way.

Just like in Westerns,
they'd ask Mikie and me
to lay our pistols on the table,
then they'd lay theirs down.
After we'd scored, they'd give us
a spoon of coke, and hash
the size of a Hershey bar.

After the Feds busted Mikie
with a pound of pure in his car,
I was so strung out on dealer's cut,
I claimed in court I saw the cops
plant dope in Mikie's trunk.
The Feds sneered, *You stupid piece of shit;*
you're not worth the time to prosecute.
They railroaded me to Rikers
where, kicking cold, I almost
bit my armpits out.

The Interview (Julio)

I'm a badass Bronx drug dealer:
six dope slingers, two enforcers,
stash of arms, chippies galore,
but with two warrants
and some of my competitors
looking to take me out,
I need to hide out for a while.

I come looking fly,
Italian leather, tie, silk shirt.
The staff wants to get to me
so they have an all-girl interview.
*You think you're a ladies' man — you ain't
nothing but a no-dick, broken-down loser.*
I sneer inside — *putas estúpidas.*

Eddie, one of the coordinators,
comes in the room and says
he's gonna chop my mop,
I bluff him. *Go ahead,* I say,
take my hair, I don't care.

So instead he makes me stand on a chair
and sing a song. He doesn't know
I'm into doo-wop.
I sing "What's Your Name," by Don and Juan.
"Sad Girl," by Joe Bataan.
"To Be With You," by Joe Cuba.

The broads don't say a word,
Eddie's bested.
I ease into the program.

Forty-Eight Hours (Holly)

I've squirmed on this chair for days,
should have never told the staff
I'd been playing leapfrog,
going from program to program with my mother,
how I hocked her rabbit coat and she locked me out,
went to Daytop Village, but, sick
of being called a junkie slut in groups,
only stayed a week.

Should never have let them know
my mother felt sorry for me and took me back,
but after I set my bed on fire, smoking and nodding,
she tossed me out again and I went to Phoenix House
but couldn't take slaving 15 hours a day in the kitchen,
cooking for 70 starving dopefiends, left in a week.

I teamed up with a girlfriend and we scammed guys
into thinking they were getting sex, then ran off
with their money, until two of them wised up
and beat the shit out of me in the back seat of their car –
I had to jump into traffic to keep from getting killed.

After kicking for three days at my aunt's,
my mother dropped me off at Logos, showed me
a warrant for the Rockefeller Program, promised
I'd do five years if I split.

The staff said I had to earn their trust
before they'd accept me, threw in my face
how I'd just split from two TCs.
But it was going to be 48 hours. I couldn't stand

my own stench. I'd only been allowed
three times to get up and use the bathroom,
and for food I'd been given stale scraps of bread
with peanut butter – and no jelly.
Everyone was so mean to me. I could't stop crying.
Please, please, let me come in, take a shower,
get some sleep, talk to somebody.

White Uncle Tom

It's a night-dark November morning.
I'm at the bottom of a stairway
somewhere in the South Bronx
at a drug program called Logos,
waiting for an interview.
My face has an orange sheen
like axle grease, I shiver
from the icy drafts
blowing through my golf jacket,
the only outer garment I own.

My bony ass is sore
from sitting on a wooden bench.
I want to split but remember:
ripping off students' books
while they sit in the cafeteria,
selling my father's stamp collection,
OD'ing on a rooftop,
carried down by dopefiends,
arms pinned behind my back,
hands tearing at my wallet,
my shirt, my shoes.

I think about waking up
with red ants in my marrow,
racing to the toilet,
vomit running through my nose,
the lump of shit in my throat.

Two hours go by,
I'm faint, vision blurred.
I want to leave but Nilsa warned me
– no more chances –
if I don't get into Logos,
she's gone for good.
I hear whispers, laughter,
the echo of a piano and vibraphone,
a voice singing
... *ratón, el ratón!*

People go up and down the stairs
staring at me. I ask somebody
for a smoke, they look away.

Finally, a man comes –
sheared hair, missing teeth.
Follow me, he says.
What took so long? I ask.
*We're a family here; we want to see
how bad you want to get in.*

In the interview I tell
a woman with a scar across her face
how I'd done social work in East Harlem.
I tell a Black man with an eye patch
how I lost my moorings.
I tell an Italian guy with a withered hand,
I can't take it anymore.

The woman shouts: *Liar, loser!*
The Black guy calls me a racist,
the Italian says I'm a white Uncle Tom.
My interviewers stand up,
leave the room.

I have no money,
no place to go.
I debate running
out the door, throwing myself
under a bus.

I hear branches bang
against the windows.
It's beginning to rain.
In two days
it will be Thanksgiving.

Car Crash in Ridley Park

I'm in a Chevy ragtop
with four classmates,
heads groggy
on cheap wine and bum weed.

Lunatic is behind the wheel
haggling us for gas money
when a tow truck runs a red light
and plows into our side.

Screams roil the air.
I leap over a crumpled door
and drop bottles and hash pipes
down a sewer drain.

The police open their pads
and record our side of the story:
college boys on their way to the library.
The trucker claims the sun blinded him.

Lunatic finds a lawyer who says
don't sweat the lack of injuries,
and sends us to a doctor who makes us
sign a mountain of medical forms.

Before getting my settlement check,
I have to show up in a Philly courtroom
with two burly escorts from Logos,
my South Bronx drug program.

I'm banned from talking
with my pothead pals,
who yuck it up like they
smoked a kilo of Maui Waui.

Back in rehab, the director
tells me to give up the check –
a down-payment
towards saving my life.

Thanksgiving

without turkey, 1969.
The best we can do
is bodega-hustled cold cuts,
stale French bread, canned apricots.

The rain hasn't let up all day.
The staff schedules extra groups
to sop up the self-pity that seeps
through the house.

It's evening and a bunch of us
just finished the kitchen detail:
washing dishes, cleaning the table,
taking out the trash.

We're stretched out on the floor.
Nobody has smokes – not even rollies –
when Betty starts singing the lead
to "Long Lonely Nights,"
by Lee Andrew & the Hearts.
Victor takes tenor; I add bass.

Julio kicks off "Lonely Teardrops,"
by Jackie Wilson; Sean joins,
along with Georgie and me.
Before we're finished, Betty croons
Little Anthony and the Imperials'
"Tears on My Pillow," our voices
in tune, harmony tight.

We're on autopilot when Betty
jumps up, mixes cornmeal, water,
a little salt, pepper,
molds the batter into cakes,
fries them in a greasy skillet,
serves them like communion wafers.

The Great Him

After he was hailed in City Hall
as Cub Scout of the year.

After he sold nude photos
of his stepmother.

After his science project
on pharmaceuticals
won first prize in junior high school.

After he drew swastikas
on the blackboard of his Hebrew class.

After he forfeited a scholarship to Yale
for burglarizing drug stores.

After he ODed on barbiturates
in a draft board bathroom.

After he was thrown out
of the U.S. Narcotics Farm in Kentucky
for filching methadone.

After he enrolled in Synanon
to dodge prison for check forgery.

After he became a counselor
and made residents deal with their "shit"
by cleaning septic tanks.

After he exhibited photos of residents
in an open coffin
who left Synanon without permission.

After he resigned
when the director wouldn't declare him
cured after five years clean time.

After he was acclaimed
as the guru of Acumen,
a Brooklyn commune of headshrinkers.

After he married Sarah Wiggens,
a Daughter of the American Revolution.

After he built three drug programs
in the Bronx called Logos.

After he began to be revered
as the Great Him.

After he bought an amber Alfa Romeo,
an emerald Porsche.

After he junketed through Latin America
collecting pre-Columbian art.

After he was appointed an Associate
at Albert Einstein School of Medicine.

After he finagled funding
to buy 50 acres of land in upstate New York.

After he foreswore the rehab field
to forge a utopian empire.

My Roommate: Crip the Creeper

He spent most of his time in the bathroom.
At night, back against the wall,
handkerchief to his face,
he'd mop slime
from his eyes, nose, mouth.

Twenty years my senior,
Mel treated me like a kid,
a dopey, naïve kid just starting
the narco game. He told his story
in nightly installments.

After a drill bit broke off in his leg
during a routine operation
in a colored hospital in Florida,
he limped to the nickname *Crip*.

At Bethune-Cookman College,
he had aspirations of becoming
the Black Tennessee Williams.
His leg never healed right,
the pain driving him
to use Dilaudid, drugstore horse.

Soon he discovered that heroin
killed the pain better. To support
his habit, he dealt from a bar
until tipped off by a cop
who dated his cousin,
that he better fly the coop.

He went underground in Roxbury,
Boston, gigged as a doorman
at a Playboy Club, doing double duty
as a dope-slinger, raking in some
heavy bread, until his own habit
spun him out of control.

Then he morphed into Crip the Creeper,
the old Black guy with the frog-like lids
who nobody paid any mind to.
He could pull the silver out of your teeth
if you slept with your mouth open.

Wearing a janitor's uniform,
he'd mastermind robberies
in warehouses, executive suites,
jewelry shops; was the most
sought-out hustler in the doper set,
the cat who could be counted on
for the best stings, the best
fences, the best get-high.

In a cab, two pimps, Snake and Shark,
gave him a stack of bills to score an ounce.
They sat in the back, Snake on one side,
Shark on the other, Mel in the middle.
The pimps argued over who threw
in the most money, anger building
until they pulled knives.
Mel raised his hands to shield
his face as Snake and Shark
stabbed at each other.
By the time they tumbled out of the cab,
Mel's mitts would need dozens of stitches.

That didn't stop him from taking off
with their money, and the next day he fled
Boston and stayed with his aunt in Harlem.
When she died he became homeless
and ended up in Logos.
After he kicked his oil burner,
Mel said he was working on a play
called "A Street Life Called Desire."

The Great Him II

Logos hadn't been open six months
when I slid in *greasy as a pork chop,* you said.
At meetings you'd flash five fingers
– *five years of being clean*, you'd boast –
sneering at anything I had to say, declaring
I still had *blood dripping down my arms.*

In your office you had a chandelier
that covered half your ceiling, teakwood
shelves for your Mayan funeral pottery,
a red leather-framed window facing
the parking spot for your new Porsche,
a wall-to-wall tropical fish tank.

Once, you found a fly floating in the water,
said the maintenance crew lacked
peripheral vision,
made us scrub all the walls
with a toothbrush to perfect
our powers of concentration.

Image

Daryl's barbell-sculpted biceps
wear prison-tattoo sleeves,
naked women shimmy
when he moves.
His half-closed eyes beam:
What-are-you-looking-at-bitch-
I'll-bust-your-mothafuckin'-ass.

We try to break him down,
show him his hard-rock image
keeps him from facing his real self,
the frightened little boy who hurts
so bad he can't live without drugs.

Fuck off! I'm only here
because my parole officer said
it's either Logos or jail.

A month goes by; the Great Him
gets wind Daryl won't drop
his gangster front, intimidates
other residents by boasting
he's good at the knuckles game.

The staff calls him in,
orders him to wear a dress,
curtsy in the hallway when
he passes a male resident, sing
"My Guy" at morning meeting.

Daryl charges out,
slams the front door behind him.
A week later news filters back:
gunned down
during a botched bank robbery.

Logos: In the Beginning There Was the Word

Nicknamed The Atomic Reactor,
Holly's tongue crackles:
Why me? Back off! Bullshit!
when coordinators give her a pull-up.
She pays for her defiance
on the weekends, among
the greasy bubbles of the dishpan.

Sweet Moments (Carlota)

Willis Avenue, The Bronx

I used to love to go to the Casino,
watch a dozen cartoons, "Flash Gordon,"
"Tarzan," and three movies,
bite off the top of a wax stick candy
squeeze out the juice – cherry was my favorite –
and chew the tubes.

Later, drug dealers poured liquid
methedrine into the cut-down candy sticks
hawked them as *bombitas* – *bams* for short.
On a rooftop overlooking the Casino
I'd cold-shake a bam with cooked heroin
and shoot up a speedball delight.

Logos: Principle of Order and Knowledge

Seth lived in his parents' building,
painted everything in his basement
apartment blue: walls, chairs, couches,
lampshades, light bulbs, a tombstone,
a plot made of wood, a bent spoon.
When his mother balked at giving him
his cop money, Seth threatened suicide.

Barry

Back in the day, Barry said, white junkies
were mostly Jews, turned on to smack
by jazz musicians or their hangers-on.

Like him, a wannabe sax player
who used dope to finesse his sound,
imitating the cats around him.

Chasing the bag became his only tune.
Busted in Chicago, Detroit,
Cleveland, East Harlem.

At the 42nd Precinct, a social worker
visiting the drunk tank recruited him
into Phoenix House.

His quick wit won over the honchos,
and in time he became the head
of two Phoenix facilities.

He fell for a new resident;
after she used, he used.
Women are my downfall.

The Great Him lured Barry
from detox to Logos,
exempted him from grunt work.

Two months later Barry lorded it
over interviews, encounter groups,
wailed on his sax again.

Said he knew my type, ran over me
like a lawnmower, shredding my words
as middle-class cover-ups.

He banned me from pumping iron,
said I had to reach into my guts,
avoid cheap ways to feel good.

His room was the hip hang-out
banned me, dubbed me "The Pimple,"
told me to squeeze off.

Barry had the hots for a newbie.
When she split, he split. I remember
he boasted he got high with Bird and Trane.

No Kitchen Kitty (Sarah)

You were no lady back then
when broke and needing a fix

you'd hail a cab and from the back seat
press a spoon to the driver's head

scream you'd blow his brains out
if he didn't give up the day's earnings.

Crown of Thorns

His name was Moisés – Moses in English –
and with his scruffy beard, sunburnt skin,
and passionate patter,
he could pass for a Hebrew prophet.

He swung into Logos
on crutches
and hadn't been there a hot minute
before he told us about the pins
the doctors had put in his toes.
He was kicking cold turkey
and in between retching and the runs,
he let us look at his feet
with their wiry protuberances
resembling porcupine spines.

He gave us the scoop:
he'd been on his knees under a stairwell
on Saint Ann's Avenue
shooting up some Mexican Brown
when he ODed and fell over backwards,
cutting off the circulation
in his lower legs and feet,
causing his toes to wither
from near-gangrene.

Logos had only been open
a couple of months,
and while the residents patched the roof,
plastered the ceilings,
repaired the stairways,

doing what they could
to get the ramshackle tenement
into livable shape,
Moses rested on his crutches
and boasted of his plumbing skills,
carpentry skills, electrical skills;
swore that as soon as he got his Medicaid card
and had his operation
he'd show us how to rehab our slum building
from basement to attic.

Two days after his surgery
while we were asleep
Moses packed up his bags
and disappeared.
He took with him the one-speaker stereo,
the power drill, tool box, wrench set;
cleared out the Thanksgiving turkeys
donated by the local A&P,
removed the clock
from the group room wall.

The staff struck back,
turned our material loss
into a therapeutic gain.
The silver pins found at the bottom
of Moses' bed
were fit into the crown
of a frilly gold bonnet
residents were made to wear
as a learning experience
if caught taking
an unauthorized cracker, cookie,
or cup of coffee.

Rehab Gab

I was tore up from the floor up.

I only had two brain cells left
and they were waving goodbye to each other.

From Park Avenue to park bench.

If you don't change, you'll be begging change.

She was your girl one day
and everybody's girl on payday.

You need a checkup from the neck up.

You're only as sick as your secrets.

Fake it to make it.

He had Peru tattooed on the side of his nose.

There's no reverse in a hearse.

Seven Reasons

Stevie shot dope 'cause
he had BO.

Eileen shot dope 'cause
her clothes were chintzy.

Greg shot dope 'cause
his tool was too small.

Lynn shot dope 'cause
it poured on her birthday.

Josh shot dope 'cause
he spoke with a stutter.

Carol shot dope 'cause
mom jazzed the mailman.

Sten shot dope 'cause
he lost his lucky penny.

"Snaggletoothed Pervert"

the poster board reads,
dangling from David's neck
with a sketch of his face,
jagged front tooth protruding.
Please help me!
I'm so desperate
for a good feeling
I fornicated with my sister
on a coffee table.

Betty, the resident he had sex with,
is on "contract" too, her hair
stuffed into a stocking cap.
Whenever she runs into a resident,
she must expound on the difference
between immediate
and deferred gratification.

Two-hundred-pound Betty
has her sisters tittering in groups
when she talks about the dread she felt
being jazzed by a man with such a large member.

David and Betty are forbidden to talk
to each other, and when not involved
in therapy, spend their time scrubbing
and mopping floors, walls, and toilets.

David wears his sign like a badge of honor.
In a place full of horny guys,
he's the only stud who can boast
scoring in-house booty.

Squares

The drug counselors say
we're the flipside of squares.

We want what we want when we want it.
The squares defer pleasure.

We're selfish and think about me, me, me.
The squares are concerned about others.

We're chronic gripers.
The squares make the best of an imperfect world.

The counselors say we try to tear apart
everything the squares try to hold together:
family, neighborhood, business, government.

We are held in protective custody
force-fed tough love
to learn to adapt to the square world outside.

At night the TV flickers.
We see the stretchers carting the dead
off the battlefields of Vietnam,

the white faces of the national guardsmen
patrolling the Black neighborhoods of America,
the public hospitals where patients die in waiting rooms.

A spark of defiance flares in our guts.
We're tempted to curse, strike out at authority
or, better yet, run to the cop man and get fucked up.

In Memorium

To L.Z.

When I said I'd been to college,
you said, *Let him in, we could use*
some brains around here.

I had no idea who I was,
a white junkie whose crime partners
were all Black and Puerto Rican.

Your words cut deep, your eyes
deeper, as you stripped away
layers of lies.

You didn't spare yourself, shared
scenes of your junkie past, bloodied,
on your knees, behind bars.

When you spoke about your new life,
you grinned, grabbed your pot belly,
and said, *I got mines.*

An Italian from East Harlem,
your honesty and nerve
made me hope I could change.

The Meat Rack

She stood out with her dyed-black pixie hairdo,
candle-white skin, so gaunt
her eyes looked like golf balls.
Whenever I got off the subway
at 125th and Lex – my home stop –
she'd be there,
a regular among the prostitutes.

I had the typical male junkie
reaction to female addicts:
they disgusted me.
As I'd exit the station
I'd keep my head down,
making a dash past the meat rack.

In spite of my disguise
– Kangol cap, oval shades, moustache, and chin beard –
the hookers had that extra sense,
knew I was an outsider, *un blanquito*,
would come on to me like I was a trick:
¡Mira, chico, la salsa caliente!
Yo, baby, let mamma cool ya!

Five blocks away in my railroad flat,
I still wasn't free of them.
One lived in the apartment above
and I'd hear her pimp smacking her
at all hours of the day and night.

Get up off my money, bitch,
or I'll put my shoe up your ass.
The ceiling would shake, sending down
flakes of plaster, causing my neighbors
to joke that it snowed in my crib
even in the summertime.

After I entered Logos,
I was shocked to be joined weeks later
by the pixie-cut from 125th Street.
I watched her do a makeover:
new hairdo, new teeth,
a young boyfriend.
But at the end of the program
she got pregnant and went to Lincoln Hospital
– known as the Butcher Shop by locals –
to have an abortion
and, getting an anesthesia
contraindicated by her asthma,
died on the operating table.

At Ortiz's Funeral Home
on East 103rd Street,
by the black wall of the Park Avenue El,
I waited until everyone in our program
paid their respects, then joined
the whores to say goodbye.

Back in the South Bronx,
shades drawn tight,
shadows like boa constrictors,
someone said, *Shit, we're all on borrowed time.*
Still I saw traces of light
left by the pixie-cut meat-racker.

The Man Who Couldn't Feel

came to encounter groups
where people tore each other a new asshole
for leaving the top off the peanut butter jar
and when they asked Sean how he felt,
he'd say, *Sorry, I can't feel anything.*

People broke down, shamed
by peddling their bodies, their parents'
wedding rings for a bag of dope.
Sean blinked his blue eyes.
Sorry, I can't feel anything.

Julio said, *You have a gorgeous blonde
who drives a Caddy, gives you money,
and calls you every day. What's up?*
It don't matter, Sean repeats.
I can't feel anything.

Eddie, the group leader, laughed.
Sean's the only honest one here,
he said, pounding the coffee table.
*The only real feeling the rest of you
have is when you have to take a shit.*

Delicacies

The staff says it's my turn
to hustle food donations;
the brothers and sisters are hungry.

I head for Bronx's Little Italy,
Arthur Avenue, where grandpa's
family lived thirty years ago.
People take pity when I say

I'm an ex-dope addict
struggling to stay off the stuff.
I return with caponata, artichokes,
olives, boxes of rigatoni, penne.

The mostly Black and Puerto Rican
residents have little taste
for Italian food. I have a field day
feasting on delicacies.

After a few days the merchants
grumble, but the staff says I can't
take "no" for an answer, and growling
stomachs thunder in my head.

I go to Titelli Brothers,
crates stacked like fortress walls,
repeat *we are a non-profit ...*
they stop me, *We gave once, twice, three times*

now beat it. I persist. Mr. Titelli
wears a coral horn around his neck,

picks up a five-pound can of tomatoes,
Scram or I'll bounce this off your head.

I clear out, head for the Dominican-owned
bodegas; they give milk, bread, eggs,
potatoes; *Vayas con Dios.*

The Staff of Life (Georgie)

It's my turn to do the bread
run at Ward's Bakery.

Waiting for the loaves, I swipe
two cookies from the counter.

Can't hold the guilt, cop out
in a group, a general meeting

is called, I'm chewed-out
by my bothers and sisters,

given a month-long contract.
Made to wear a crayon-

scrawled sign: *I'm a thief*
whose stealing jeopardizes

the very bread
that feeds my family.

What Carlota Wants

Counselors talk *treatment goals,*
working together. What she wants is:

no memory of her mother
puking on herself in a police cell,

no memory of her mother
balling tricks in the bed next to her,

no memory of her mother
stabbing a boyfriend over drug money,

no memory of her mother
stiff as a frozen fish in the alleyway.

Callus

Discipline at Logos is a joke.
After four years at military college,
rising at dawn, GI-ing my room,
being on time for meetings is a cinch.

I avoid jackpots – trouble with the staff
for disrespect, disobedience;
I don't get verbal haircuts,
learning experiences, contracts.

Friday night, I'm set to see Nilsa,
when the assistant director says,
You're in the dishpan for the weekend.
Why? I ask incredulously.

I want you to deal with the feelings,
put a callus on your belly, learn how
to take life's bitter blows without
making a beeline to the pusher.

SIDING WITH
THE ENEMY

Salt Shot (Julio)

Back then I spent more time on rooftops
than I did on level ground.
Having learned how to pick locks
and jump cars while in prison,
I no longer had to sweat my get-high money.
Just a break-in or car heist a week
– sometimes I could stretch it to ten days –
kept the hype sticks coming.

Those were the golden days
of the buck-fifty caps of ass-kicking *caballo*.
I had a good fence
and kept feeding him cars, TVs, stereos
– and when Little Johnny was with me –
we'd even wheel in washing machines, stoves,
refrigerators, and entire dining room sets.

The good times just kept comin'
'til I shot some killer coke and fell out
on a rooftop on Tiffany Avenue.
Little Johnny remembered the stories
the old-timers told
of reviving ODs with salt shots
and left me on the tar paper
to go to the bodega
for a cardboard canister of Diamond Crystal.

In a rusty olive jar lid,
he cooked a saltwater solution
and squeezed off two hefty hits
in both upper arms.

When I didn't come to,
he waved down a cop,
who ran to the roof,
slung me over his shoulder,
and hauled me down to Lincoln Hospital.

Woke up in the ER,
arms puffed up like they'd been pounded
with rifle butts.
The docs said I'd have to wait a few weeks
before they could fix me up.
I stayed home, watching TV, both arms
festering from apple-sized abscesses.
Finally the docs strapped me down,
told me to bite down on some cotton wadding
and, without anesthesia,
cut out the rotting tissue
from the twin pus pockets.

I never hit myself off
with a hype stick again.
Coke went up my nose,
not in my veins.
When my pards asked me
about the ice-cream scoop craters
in my arms,
I'd throw out my chest,
brag I'd been hit by shotgun blasts
during my gang-banging days.

Goldfish and Gorilla Biscuits

When he entered Logos,
he suffered from seizures
– his brother called it *flapping* –
and he dragged his left leg as he walked.

An athlete at Clinton High School,
his fancy flips on the high bar
and crashing blocks on the hockey court
won him the nickname Johnny Ace.

He loved playing daredevil
at 16, following in his brother's footsteps,
started using H.
No sidesteps for me, he boasted,
I went from malt liquor to mainlining.

Then he banged Tuinals, Seconals,
finally overdosing on the King Kong
of gorilla biscuits – Cibas –
ending up in a coma for two weeks,
damaging the part of his brain
controlling equilibrium.

The day he arrived I heard loud voices
and saw him on the bathroom floor,
foam pouring out of his mouth,
his body convulsing like a jackhammer.

Since nobody wanted to bunk
with a spastic, I took pity on him
and agreed to be his roommate.

I pushed him to see a physical therapist,
take Dilantin. Six months later,
he walked without a limp,
worked out on the chinning bar.

In the encounter groups,
the Ace always went for his best shot,
and in spite of my entreaties
to pull his punches with the staff,
called the Great Him *a BB-balled emperor.*

From then on he couldn't move up,
couldn't become a cook, or expeditor,
or work on the acquisition team.
Instead he remained in maintenance,
personally in charge of the Great Him's
wall-to-wall goldfish tank,
teeming with fantails, veil tails,
moors, orandas, lionheads.

Three times a day the Ace
had to check glass clarity, air pumps,
water temperature, fecal accumulations,
and the chemical filtration system.
A week didn't go by without the Ace
pleading for a transfer,
but the staff laughed at him.

One day I heard the Great Him shrieking
and ran towards his office.
Johnny Ace came strolling out,
a chipped-tooth smile on his face.
I'm getting a mop, he said;
there's been an accident.
Inside, water spurted in the air,

tubes lay around unconnected,
fish wiggled on the carpet floor.

Charging him with gross negligence,
the Great Him had the Ace's head shaved,
ordered him to wear a sign around his neck
twenty-four hours a day
fringed with toilet paper,
reading, *I'm a puckering asshole.*

The Ace balked, packed his bags
– I begged him to stay – and left.
A week later, his brother stopped by,
drowsy on methadone,
reporting the Ace was gobbling Cibas,
head gashed from flapping, and hobbling
on a cut-down hockey stick.

Dopefiend Hustle # 72: The Grim Reaper (Sarah)

After a three-day bender, I return to work
and tell my boss my brother died.

I dodge my parole officer for three months,
then phone to say my father died.

When my grandmother dies I forge her signature
and keep cashing her social security checks.

At Frankie's wake I rifle through his aunts'
pocketbooks while they pray in front of his casket.

I work the N line with a McDonald cup
begging for money for my daughter's burial expenses.

I use my dead uncle's birth certificate
to get my hands on his unclaimed veterans benefits.

I beat Sammy for two kilos and arrange for a crimie
to spread the rumor I died falling off a rooftop in Frisco.

Dopefiend Hustle # 132: Playing the Christers (Seth)

Every Christer worth his cross is stuck on the scenario
of the great sinner who becomes the great saint.

I tell the minister I hear God's voice command me:
Put down the spike, the cooker, lead a sanctified life.

The pastor introduces me to his flock. They donate
clothes, food, a place to lay up, even pocket money.

I scourge myself in public, beg for forgiveness,
preach to the hardcore blasphemers.

I'm the hottest ticket at prayer meetings, Sunday service,
church picnics, fundraisers.

Everyone wants me to meet their virgin daughters,
straighten out their wayward sons.

Then the day comes when the faithful realize I've robbed
the rectory, maxed out their kids' credit cards
   – disappeared.

Family Room

Sixty people in the room.
I can't look at Carlota,
standing in a garbage barrel,
hair stuffed into a stocking cap,
eyes glassy with tears.

After splitting Logos
turning a trick
with a pawnshop owner,
the dope didn't do anything for her.
She missed her roommates,
had no place to stay.

The Great Him walks up to Carlota,
Family, she says she's sorry.
She wants us to take her back.
What do you say?

Balled-up tissue paper
fills the air.
Fuck her!
Let her peddle more ass
on the street corner!
We don't want no junkie whores!

The director smiles at Carlota.
What do you have to say for yourself?
Family, I swear
to Papá Dios ...
I'll do anything.

I close my eyes,
remember visiting her family
on Brook Avenue
after her retarded brother burned to death
in an apartment fire;
her father drunk,
her mother dressed in white,
black crosses painted on the kitchen wall.

What does the family say?
the Great Him shouts.
No easy grace!
Dress her up like a puta!
Let her scrub toilets for three months!
Welcome back, bitch!

Death of a Sobertone (Georgie)

Two weeks after he left Logos,
I got the call.
He's dead! his mother hollered,
James is dead!
Crash! She hung up the phone.

He'd been found by some
cardboard boxes near a prostitute's stroll
alongside Bruckner Boulevard.
The police report read: *Death*
by heroin overdose.

Our first meeting: his shirt
with the ripped pocket,
his wide hips and rough laughter
that made his belly roll,
the burn scar cutting a swath
alongside his high Afro.

After six months of therapy,
he still wouldn't say how he'd gotten burned,
though a rumor claimed he'd been blow-torched
after robbing a drug dealer.

I came up with the idea of forming a trio
after hearing James sing
"Sittin' On the Dock of the Bay."
I took tenor, Roger baritone, and James,
with the most soulful voice, took lead.
Our fellow residents dubbed us the Sobertones.

We sang: "Try a Little Tenderness,"
"Pain in My Heart,"
"Mr. Pitiful."
At house parties, barbecues,
morning meetings, the residents cheered us on,
found any excuse to hear us harmonize.

But the Great Him snubbed us,
claimed we should raise our octave
above street-corner crooning and pabulum poetry,
soar with jazz and the classics.

Then the Great Him did a room run,
found a pair of James' pants
with bologna slices in the pockets.
He demanded an example be made
of James' dopefiend gluttony,
had his head shaved,
ordered him to sleep in the bathtub
wearing pink gloves and a pig's mask.

When James beefed about sleeplessness,
Roger and I were ordered to hold open the front door
while the Great Him threw him out,
tossing his suitcase across Washington Avenue.

I swallowed hard, remembered Otis Redding's
plane going down in a lake in Wisconsin,
worried how the show would go on.

Hats Off

Logos dogma: dopers can't handle feelings,
they act them out by getting stupid, crazy, stoned.
Groups are medicine, a siphon for poisons,
catalyst for long-term healing.
Anything goes in groups but bloodshed, the staff
curbs "rat-packing" – pounding on one person.
In groups, the staff take their "hats off," can be
targets of the same raw emotions as residents.

Sean's girl, Lily, is a model, studied Gestalt, primal
scream therapy, yoga, hypnosis, psychodrama.
She attends family and friends groups,
The Great Him oversees every Tuesday.
Lily skewers him for threatening to make
residents homeless if they challenge him.
The Great Him orders her to shut up or leave.
The louder he snarls, the more she hacks him to pieces.
*You want to gag me because you're not man
enough to face the truth,* she snaps; *You're a fraud!*
We're all in shock; we've never seen the Great Him
fumble for words, lose his cool.
The Great Him bans Lily from Logos, warns Sean
he'll be living under a bridge if he doesn't dump her.

Siding with the Enemy

We finish a marathon –
26 hours of group therapy.
Seth slumps in a corner
blubbering, pain gushing
like a broken water main.

After plumbing our depths,
the group leader, Papa Jim,
leads us to the Bronx Zoo.
We clown around with monkeys,
hippos, seals. On the return,
Papa Jim takes a shortcut
through the Italian neighborhood.

We strut down the street,
arm in arm, white, Black,
Puerto Rican, singing:
"Only the Strong Survive,"
"Raindrops Keep Fallin' on My Head."

Bottles fly, exploding
on the streets, sidewalks,
people pour out of cafés,
social clubs, and stores.
Get the hell out of here!
A few Logos brothers rip off
car antennas, ready to rumble.
I jump in front. *Are you crazy?*
We'll get slaughtered.

A squad car screeches. The sergeant
shouts, *You can't bring a mob*
into this neighborhood,
you want a riot? He escorts us
out of the gauntlet, but two white teens
keep throwing bottles. Brian
and Georgie charge, throw bottles back.

Later, the Great Him
summons us into his office.
I peel you wet brains
off the pavement, put food
in your bellies, and for many of you —
the teeth to chew it —
and you're going to ruin
my relations with this community?

As a learning experience,
the antenna-snatchers
and bottle-tossers spend weeks
in the dishpan, busting suds.
The hotheads call me a punk
for not fighting back, a traitor
because I'm Italian.

GIL FAGIANI

Speaking Engagement

Unable to keep my throat lubed
or my legs still,
I stand in front
of an auditorium full
of rollicking black faces
at Walton High School,
where my mother graduated
thirty-three years before.
I manage to mumble
a few sentences about
the pain, the self-loathing
of my life as a drug addict,
when a girl yells,
Hey, you cute, white daddy.

Splitee (Julio)

The counselors are negative,
stuck in the past, can't see
Lady is not like my ex.
She got her AA coin
for six months of sobriety,
and when I split the program,
I'll help raise her kids.

I'm tight again with my Lord,
He tells me I can make it.
The preacher says I'm the star
at Friday night Bible lessons.

The counselors rag me
about my blackouts, ODs, jail time;
they only want my rent check
and food stamps.
It's time to think about me!

I'm sick of being cooped up,
need to stay away
from negative people,
land a nine-to-five, live
a righteous life with Lady.

The Feast

Nine months in Logos,
I'm at the San Gennaro Feast
with my girl Nilsa,
cousin Dom, his wife Carmen,
squeezing past food stands
along Mulberry Street,
where my grandparents lived
and my father was born.

Yesterday my roommate
split the program,
rather than accept
a weekend restriction
for talking back to the staff.

Today I'm high
on rippling accordion glissandos,
greetings exchanged in *siciliano*,
pugliese, calabrese,
air spicy with peppers and onions,
zeppoli sizzling
in three-foot vats of cooking oil.

Knowing later they will chip in
for my dinner tab,
I say *no thanks*
when Nilsa and Carmen
offer me money
for games of chance
or to pin a dollar on San Gennaro.

We eat in Puglia's,
where a fiftyish woman
in a black dress with a gold medallion
between beach ball breasts
belts out Neopolitan standards:
"Torna a Surriento," "Malafemmena."

My eyes moisten as I eat my antipasto.
I look at my cousin;
married, working, with a college diploma,
while I'm mired in memories:
face slammed into a wall by narcos,
birthday in a mental hospital,
bloody body carried down from a rooftop.

Still, I'm happy today; it's just that
the singer's every note grabs me in the gut
and now the tears are flowing.
Dom half-covers his face with his napkin.
I excuse myself, hustle off to the bathroom.
When I return, the music has stopped.
Soon I'll start school,
find a job, move in with Nilsa.

The Great Him Muses

We refuse to integrate our members into the decay and corruption of the outer society. We're creating an autonomous community based on truth and self-purification.

We'll call this city in the sun *Logosburg*. This is why we purchased what had been the second largest-hotel in the Catskills. We must abandon the large urban areas because they host the culture of death in its most concentrated forms.

We'll stop accepting poor inner-city drug addicts. We'll recruit the most advanced elements from the straight world, who can benefit from our cleansing environment, contribute to its dynamic.

Logosburg will be governed by prophets, visionaries, with uncontaminated minds, who will invent new ways of doing things. We'll offer 24-hour forums dedicated to philosophy, science, the arts. We'll grow our own crops, raise animals, farm fish, develop a dairy. The profits will ensure financial independence.

We'll sponsor intensive therapeutic weekends for high rollers, whose money will defray our expenses. Outsiders will break our door down to get in. We'll represent the new millennium, a 21st century Promised Land.

The Oracle Room (Georgie)

The Great Him says six of us
have attained the highest octave
of cosmic wisdom at Logos.
He calls us Oracles,
designates a spacious
veranda as "The Oracle Room,"
a forum for philosophy,
spiritual reflection,
sanctuary from the outer world
– including the paid staff.

Caught up in the spirit of openness,
I dedicate myself to decorating
the walls of the Oracle Room.
Using an encyclopedia as a guide,
I paint Egyptian hieroglyphics,
a huge sun shooting out flames,
each with a zodiac sign.

My work wins praise from my peers
plus the staff; I labor up to
sixteen hours a day to create
beauty and enchantment.
When I arrive early one morning,
brushes in hand, I discover all
my art work has been painted over.

Later, the Great Him confronts me,
says I'm grandiose, tripping out,
that I'm not at Logos
to be Van Gogh, but to learn how

to keep a spike out of my arm,
the drool off my lips.

The Prophet: Longing is a Torrent Rushing to the Sea

The Great Him promises to put
senior residents on payroll, but keeps
hiring his cronies from Synanon.
After a year of free labor and signing over
our welfare checks, we get five dollars
of W.A.M. – walk-around money.
Our mouths reek of burnt coffee.

Omen

Staff drones: *Logos saved your life.*
Clean for a year, I agree.
But I'm sick of residents
reamed-out as *morons,*
men with sheared heads, women
standing in garbage cans,
rat-packing psychic massacres.

Nilsa rents a studio apartment
on Burnside Avenue,
invites me to share her bed.
I dream of sex, a new life,
manning the barricades
in the South Bronx, battling
for community control –
Power to the People!

The staff berates me:
unready, ungrateful.
Mocks me for slinking off
to a woman instead of standing
on my own two feet, predicts:
relapse, jail, early death.

At dawn, carrying two
plastic bags of clothes,
I walk along the vast emptiness
of Webster Avenue
to join Nilsa,
when a gas station's gates open,
a German Shepherd charges out,
sinks its fangs into my thigh.

The Prophet: When Good is Hungry it Seeks Food even in Dark Caves

Encouraged by a psych intern,
the senior residents quit reading
spiritual tracts, pop psychology;
instead, they study the art
of guerilla warfare, run groups
based on the teachings of Fidel,
Ho Chi Minh, Mao Tse-tung,
prepare for the People's uprising.

Last Day

The coordinator is speechless
when I announce I'm leaving.
I'm an oracle – a role model –
live in a status pad on the first floor.

I've lost faith in the Great Him,
dead set against his scheme
to turn Logos into
his kingdom in the Catskills.

The coordinator's lips quiver:
What bothers me is, you've taken
so much; isn't it time
you gave something back?

You lying sack of shit, I say;
I've given my soul to this place.
The coordinator ends the group,
rushes to make a phone call.
I hug my brothers and sisters.

A SINGLE SPARK

The Spirits

I move in with Nilsa, invite Carlota and Brian to join us.
A doctor friend cajoles colleagues into letting rebel splitees
use their home addresses for food stamps, welfare checks.
More residents leave. We are The Spirit of Logos. We pick-
et in front of Logos II, call for the Great Him's ouster, a
transfer of control to senior residents who built the pro-
gram. Those who support the staff patrol the rooftop with
baseball bats, rain curses down on us, dare us to break
in. Weeks after, our ranks swell as a van full of residents
escapes from Logos III in Liberty, New York. We crash a
meeting of the Board of Estimate, demand Logos' funding
go to The S.O.L. – *the sun* in Spanish. Our bid is unan-
imously rejected. We roll from reform to Revolution, ally
with the Panthers, Young Lords, view drug addiction as
only one sign of capitalism's deadly decay. We swim with
the red tide; the poor and oppressed will rule the earth.

Walking Past the Playboy Club, 1971

We were revolutionaries at war with the rich, and nobody hated the rich as much as Georgie. A ham-fisted six-footer of working-class, Ukrainian stock, he grew up in the South Bronx and, by 10, he was on his own, after his mother died and his father ditched the family. Georgie went from dope addiction, prison, rehab, to joining the revolutionary vanguard, organizing to strip the rich of their wealth and power. Once, we were sitting on the subway, when two guys in jackets and ties entered our car. Georgie, said, *Watch this,* and stamped his feet for a good five minutes. The guys in the monkey suits looked terrified. As we got off, Georgie held his nose. *Let's get away from these stinking pigs.* I recall feeling a pang of conscience – my uncle Charlie was a lowly messenger on Wall Street, and wore a tie and jacket to his job. Later, on 59th Street, we walked by the Playboy Club. A line of men in suits stretched along the long stairways under the giant rabbit-in-tuxedo symbol. Georgie shook his fist. *Your days are numbered, pigs; when the Revolution comes, you'll be swinging from the lampposts.* I stared at two Playboy bunnies threading their way to the door, wondering if they would be treated like collaborators.

On My Way to My First Job after Rehab

Morning rush hour. I hold the door
as two women, tits half out,
squeeze into the packed subway car.

Charcoal eyeliner, chalky lipstick,
guttural voice ... *dyno shit ...*
let's cop some blow and speedball.

Next stop, one woman bolts out the car,
the other upchucks on the floor:
grits, eggs, sausages, toast.

Riders jump back, the woman
staggers into a closing door,
her friend pulls her from the outside.

I grab the crease of my pants,
shake off a blob of grape jelly.

A Single Spark

I had a soft spot for Johnny Ace
and when he'd come in the storefront
high on goofballs or dope,
I'd let him sit on the sofa in the back room
surrounded by posters of Huey P. Newton,
Che, and Mao Tse-tung.

The Ace carried a pocket tape recorder
and I'd hear him reading from one of Mao's
pamphlets: "A Single Spark
Can Start a Prairie Fire."
This is Johnny Ace broadcasting
the invincible thoughts of Chairman
Mao Tse-tung from 184th Street
in the Bronx ...

Johnny Ace knew the community,
and although he was rarely sober,
I hoped that by engaging him
in the revolutionary process,
we could sharpen the contradictions
between his defeatist dopefiend side
and his new progressive side
– with the new winning out over the old –
allowing the Ace to metamorphose
into a tribune of the North Bronx proletariat.

One day he stumbled into the storefront,
eyes half-closed, a cigarette ash
curled around his fingers,
and I handed him a leaflet blasting

the NYPD for "losing" 400 pounds
of heroin and cocaine
stored in police property rooms.

Then I went to the front office
where a man suited-up
like a Wall Street broker
pointed to Ho Chi Minh's picture
and denounced him as a counter-
revolutionary who ordered
the shooting of Vietnamese followers
of Leon Trotsky, founder of the Red
Army and polestar
of the Permanent Revolution.

Showing the Trotskyist the door,
I smelled something burning
and found the Ace in the back room
face buried in the "Cops
Push Dope" leaflet
smoke pouring out of the sofa.

After I shook the Ace out of his nod,
the two of us ran back
and forth from the bathroom,
throwing jars of water on the sofa.
The smoke still spewed out
so we lugged the sofa
out into the street,
wrenching and ripping it apart,
stamping its smoldering guts,
but the fire kept going.

The Underground Struggle (Georgie)

The doors open at 96th Street
and the white guys in suits
get ready to bolt.
I'm blocking the door
when one of them says,
I want to get off.
What's the magic word?
I say, not budging.
Excuse me, he says,
shooting a dirty look.
I turn to the crowd,
That's the trouble with their class;
they never excuse themselves
for anything they do.

Water Games

Humacao, Puerto Rico, 1971

Sunset, a blaze of purple and pink.
Nilsa takes two slugs of Bacardi,
throws the bottle into the incoming tide.
The race is on! I swim out,
grab the jug before Sean, unscrew the cap,
take a gulp, toss the bottle back into the sea.
Battling breakers, jellyfish,
lengthening shadows of dawn,
the three of us chase the green glass,
swimming and swilling until, in total darkness,
Sean flounders in the foam of the shoreline,
Nilsa passes out in the back seat of the car,
I floor the gas pedal, sink tires into the sand.

Honeymoon

We cruised
on sensual overdrive:
nearby beaches,
cooling trade winds,
fried fish and *arepas,*
candied papaya,
rum, and more rum.

There were no tourists
in Guyama, Puerto Rico,
no *norteamericanos.*
We went to bed,
skin tingling
from the tropical sun,
the *co-qui* of tree frogs
providing a cradlesong.

Then the floorboards shook
and we heard snorts
loud as lions' roars.
Fearing our flesh
would be shredded
by giant talons,
or our faces eaten off,
we clutched each other
under mosquito netting.

A pig was slaughtered –
juicy chunks of pork,
crispy skin,
blood sausage,
rum, and more rum.

The Battle of Bean Hill

Strung out on barbiturates, *beanheads* were considered the lowest of the low by other junkies. Over the years, the area near Fordham Road in the Bronx where they hung out came to be known as *Bean Hill*. A regular among the beanheads, Tommy O'Toole dragged his left foot when he walked, having destroyed it when he jumped out of a two-story hospital window the day after his broken leg had been put into a cast. The daring leap had been done in quest of his beloved beans. Besides being a major consumer of beans himself, Tommy doubled as a small-time dealer and, to safeguard his stash, pioneered the practice of "keistering," wrapping his beans in tin foil and plastic, and inserting them up his rectum. Two-Fingers Frank Galuzzo was another beanhead regular. He picked up his nickname after he got stoned and stuck his hand into a radiator fan. Bad blood flowed between Two-Fingers and Tommy, Two-Fingers insisting that Tommy gave him a short count whenever he bought a baker's dozen. *Da muddafucka,* Two-Fingers used to gripe, *thinks 'cuz I'm missing a couple of digits that I can't count past seven.* Just before Christmas, a group of holiday shoppers crowded into a coffee shop on Bean Hill, when Tommy and Two-Fingers began to argue outside. Both were "beaned" to the gills and, as they cursed each other, wobbled like their joints were made of rubber. They threw punches, arms moving as if underwater. After Tommy took a left hook to the nose that drew blood, he staggered backwards and pulled off his thick brass-buckled belt. He lashed Two-Fingers with the belt, and although he couldn't swing with much force, the buckle end of the belt left a meshwork of bloody streaks across Two-Fingers' face. The blood dripping down his face didn't phase Two- Fingers, and he kept throwing slow-motion punches Tommy's way. Finally, Tommy dropped his belt, and from a holster strapped to his ankle, pulled out a linoleum knife with a wicked, curved blade. Coffee shop diners cringed in anticipation of Two-Fingers being hacked into hamburger meat. No sooner had Tommy unsheathed the knife when it fell out of his hand. As he bent down to pick it up, Two-Fingers kneed him in the face, sending him sprawling across the sidewalk. *Look at da muddafucka now,* he beamed, resting one of his feet on Tommy's bean-keistered butt, and waving his two-fingered hand in the air like he was flashing a victory sign.

Flapping

Thump! Thump!
I don't believe it.
Is that sound coming from the living room?
It's four o'clock in the morning.
Maybe I'm hearing things.

Thump! Thump!
No, it's happening again.
Johnny "Ace" is having a goddam seizure.
All night long, my roommate Sean and I
have been dealing with them, each one stronger
and longer than the last,
doing our best to keep the Ace from splitting his skull
or strangling on his tongue.

I open my eyes and look next to me.
Thank God, Nilsa is still asleep.
She'll kill me if she wakes up.
She's already pissed at me for turning
our love nest into a commune
and playing "revolutionary savior"
while she's staring down the smelly mouths
of welfare recipients, working
as an assistant at a dental clinic.

When the Ace stopped by, banged up on beans,
his forehead gashed, his lips shredded,
why did I feel sorry for him and let him stay over?
I should have called his brother.
What does his brother call his seizures?
Flapping – that's what he calls them.
No, his brother is fed up with his shenanigans.

Maybe I should have packed him up in a cab
and sent him to his parents' house.
But his mother called me last week
and said, "Oh dear, what should I do?
Johnny just broke a vase over his father's head."
No, his parents have had it with him too.

Thump! Thump!
"Gil!"
Oh shit, that's Sean.
He wants me to get up and help him.
"Gil! Gil! "
Why can't he take care of him?
Hell, I'm a married man.
Sean has a shamrock tattoo on his hand,
just like the Ace does,
Let Sean take care of him; they're both spud-fuckers.

Thump! Thump!
"Gil! Gil! Gil!"
Fuck you, Sean, I need my shut-eye!

Suddenly Nilsa sits up,
whacks me in the head with her pillow.
"Damn you, I gotta go to work in two hours;
didn't I tell you to keep your skid friends out of here?"

Thump! Thump!
"Gil!"
My feet hit the cold floor.

Vermin

I wake up to the rattle of the iron pole of my police lock as Nilsa leaves to go to work at a medical office, where she says the doctor smells so badly of curry I never have to sweat her taking him up on his standing offer to quit her job and live with him. I'd been putting down Bacardi all night with some local lumpens, confident they'd soon join our revolutionary commando operation and rid Bickford's, on Fordham Road, of some vermin dealing death drugs to the People. My eyes feel like thumb tacks and my throat is as dry as a desert bone. I get out of bed, wrinkle my nose at the odor of dirty sheets, stare in disgust at the dust balls the size of mop heads, the dishes with the paint-hard residue. Nilsa's angry words hang in the air: *If you can't bring home a paycheck, at least clean the house!* She's right. Only a male with zero consciousness, a real reactionary, expects women to do all the housework, especially one socking the clock 50 hours a week with a Medicaid quack. But the needs of the Revolution: the meetings, the rallies, the newspaper sales – I'm behind in my newspaper sales – leave me with barely time to wash my face. I start coughing, spot a half-full glass of OJ. It may contain rum, a bit of the hair of the dog that bit me might be just what the doctor calls for. I toss the juice into my mouth. Furry legs and feelers tickle my cheeks, my tongue. I bolt into the bathroom, coughing roaches into the crapper.

Behind the Paradise Theater

I met Brian bunking in the basement
at Logos, wearing a Lone Ranger mask,
his hair shaved off,
the word "THIEF" scrawled
in pink lipstick across his forehead.
He'd been caught shooting dope
with money he'd lifted from the staff kitty,
and after begging not to be thrown out,
agreed to his basement-bound,
month-long therapeutic contract.

With his large, flour-white head,
Brian looked like Casper the Ghost,
and it spooked me that he accepted his contract
since he was one of Brooklyn's baddest,
a righteous fiend who didn't bankroll
his habit by panhandling
or sneaking dollars from Mommy's purse,
but pushed his way into people's apartments
and commandeered cars at gunpoint.

I had no choice, Brian told me.
Just before I was paroled here,
I ripped some coons off for six cartons of cigarettes.
If I get sent get back to Rikers, I'm dead.

After we left the program, I noticed
Brian always got into beefs with Black people.
He'd bump into them in the street,
rant at Haitian cab drivers,
and often I had to pull him away from a situation
that was spiraling towards fisticuffs.

Once we went to a party on Walton Avenue,
behind the Loew's Paradise Theater.
The area had changed from an Irish neighborhood
to mixed Black and Latino.
Two Irish sisters, both shabbily dressed,
with acne-splotched faces, and decayed teeth,
were throwing birthday parties for their Black boyfriends,
who were both handsome and dapper.

Maybe he felt personally provoked
because he was Irish himself,
but as Brian watched the two sisters
snuggle up to their Black boyfriends
and say, like sisters from the Deep South:
Sho'nuff!
Ain't that the truth!
You best better believe it!
I could see his head glowing like a giant light bulb.

Later I heard him arguing
with one of the sisters in a bedroom,
where the peeling paint looked like ocean waves.
What are you talking about? he raged.
You're white, that's reality; you're white, just like me!
The sister's face turned just as red as Brian's
and, through her rotten teeth, she spat out,
Yeah, well, not by choice!

Tupperware Party, 1973

We enter the East Harlem apartment.
I expect loud music and spinning bodies,
my wife's family loves to dance, dance, dance.
Instead, her cousin Édgar ushers us
to a circle of chairs in the living room.

I've downed my "party-prep" – the three Millers
and half pint of DonQ I need
before I can get on the dance floor.
I've brought a six-pack.
The last thing I want is to sit with people
who act church-service sober.

A Black man in a suit stands.
My name is Douglaston, your host for the evening.
None of my wife's cousins will make eye contact with me.
I smell a rat. Where's the party?

I give my wife a sour look.
She glares at me as I pour a beer.
Let's talk about dreams, Douglaston says.
What are your fondest dreams?
Cousin Cruz says *a big house*, his wife Carmen says
a high-paying job, Édgar throws in *a fancy car.*

I squirm. I consider myself a revolutionary,
a Red Guard, but knowing my wife is staring at me,
I bite my tongue instead of thundering:
Smash the fuckin' state! Up with the proletariat!

Douglaston shakes his head. *Why are you all so modest?*
Any of you can be President if you set your mind to it.
I look at the shades of brown surrounding me,
my wife among the darkest.
That's bullshit, I say, *ain't no way a poor person*
can be President of the U.S., especially if he's not white.

What's Going On?

That's the Revolution song,
Carlos used to say, when he heard
the opening sax solo and Marvin Gaye's voice.

In a struggle session, he tried to brain
Cookie with the standup ashtray
Sean donated to our collective –
I grabbed it from behind.

Carlos popped Cookie's cherry,
though she offered it to Sean first.
Sean talked up the iron broom of history,
scoffed at bourgeois morality,
but his balls remained in the ringer
of the Holy Mother Church.

He had my back in the ideological warfare
with Carlos and his Gang of Two.
When Carlos waved a pistol,
denounced me as a police agent,
Sean split to Orcus Island,
where he worked as a caretaker for a rich dentist.

He left his politics in the Bronx,
but slept with *The Red Book* under his pillow,
renamed his boss' twin golden retrievers
Fidel and *Mao*.

The Great Him III

Years later, Georgie told me
he caught a hard-on
seeing you on the balls of your ass
in the prospect chair of his program,
desperate to be detoxed,
fake Rolex flashing from your wrist.

Nunchakus on the Concourse (Georgie)

The Panthers preached: *Pick up the gun!*
The Young Lords pulled off
an armed takeover of a church.
As white revolutionaries,
we figured the least we could do
to help stem the fascist tide
was to arm ourselves with nunchakus
– octagonal-shaped, mahogany sticks,
bound together with nylon cord.

We'd seen their deadly effects
in dozens of Kung Fu flicks,
and a comrade named Kirk
who had martial arts training
went to Chinatown to make the score.
For five bucks a pop,
we had a weapon that could run rings
around a pig's nightstick.

Kirk taught us how to tuck
nunchakus under our arm,
whip them out with sword-like precision,
change hands between our legs,
slashing figure of eight patterns in the air
with more power than a baseball bat.

When we practiced in the schoolyard,
we brought plenty of ice cubes
because, inevitably, some comrade
would conk their elbow or knee
and be in need of a pain-numbing.

I used my nunchakus once.
My ex-girlfriend Holly's old man
had been locked up for parole violation
and in order to pay the bills,
Holly kept operating his marijuana business
out of her apartment.
One day she telephoned me in tears.
Georgie, some bastard pretending to be a customer
just robbed me of all my stash and money.

After getting a descrip of what he looked like,
I grabbed my nunchakus
and caught up with the creep
on 188th Street and the Grand Concourse.
A head higher and 50 pounds heavier,
he eyeballed the nunchakus under my arm
laughed, *What you gonna do with those things?*
Without a word,
I snapped a stick into his forehead.
He pitched back against a parking meter,
then forward, his eyes crossing
like he was about to blow breakfast on his shoelaces.

Here, man, he said,
pulling bags and bills out of his pockets.
I stood,
sharply,
nunchakus under my arms.

The Queen of Latin Soul

To Guadalupe "La Lupe" Yoli

Tito Puente breaks into a solo,
his drum sticks like sea foam
slathering the shore line.

La Lupe lifts up her dress,
bends at the edge of the stage,
breasts out, swirling a red scarf.

The crowd at Madison Square Garden
jumps to its feet, cheering.
Brian pumps his hips.

*She's sniffing coke
under her fingernails*, he yells
through his hands.

Carlota glares at her Irish husband.
They met in Logos,
and married when she got pregnant.

Let's see some beaver, Chiquita,
he yells, getting into a shoving match
with two Puerto Ricans.

Carlota grabs his arm.
You're drunk; let's go.
Fuck off!

Figures you'd side with your people,
he says, fingers in his mouth, whistling,
La Lupe blowing kisses at her fans.

Last Sightings of Johnny Ace

A rehab roommate of Johnny Ace from three decades ago sees him hunched by a garbage barrel, begging change in front of the Mosholu subway station. The train rattles above, the Ace's head slumps inches above the barrel, yellow jackets buzzing by his ears.

An ex-comrade of the Ace during his Maoist phase zooms down the Grand Concourse, Playboy bunny spinning in the wind; jams on the brakes to avoid hitting the Ace, whose back is almost parallel to the asphalt, poking forward with a cane the height of a toilet plunger.

Água-Viva

In Colina Verde,
Nilsa's hometown,
men and women of all shades
swayed together
like palm trees in the wind.

And because I was so light
and she was so dark, I thought
without the ripsaw of race, our love
would smolder with the heat
of the tropical sun.

At the *playa* for the *fiesta*
of San Juan Bautista,
the same day as my birthday,
people danced the *bomba y plena*,
shared *cervecitas* and *lechón*.

While swimming
in the turquoise water,
I suffered
a needle-like scraping
natives call *água-viva*
a jellyfish you could feel
but never see.

After she left,
accusing me
of lusting after other women,
I saw my happiness sink
into a whirlpool of razor wire.

A Doper's Lament

I miss the simple life:
one goal,
any means.

The guaranteed high
fading fears,
vanishing woes.

Turning the tables
on squares,
hustling the lames.

The luscious lingo:
horse, smack, a cotton shot,
gimmicks, speedball.

The hideout
from straight friends,
family hassles.

The free pass
on paying taxes,
raising brats.

The resurrections:
from detox to rehab,
from jail to bail.

The single standard:
dyno dope trumps
status and class.

Glossary

acquisition team, also known as hustling team: A group of clients in a therapeutic community (TC) who solicit donations.

act as if: The belief that one should imitate confidence so that, as the confidence produces success, it will generate real confidence.

bams, bombitas: Liquid methedrine.

beat dope: Severely diluted or fake heroin.

bad rapping: Talking behind somebody's back instead of confronting them directly in groups.

bean, ciba, goofball, Seconal, Tuinal: Barbiturates, downers.

Bird: Nickname for jazz saxophonist Charlie Parker.

blanquito: White person.

blow: Cocaine.

brothers and sisters: Residents of a TC.

caballo, dugee, H, horse, scag, smack: Heroin.

chipping: Occasional drug use.

Chiva-Chiva, Maui-Waui, Sinsemilla: High-grade marijuana.

cold shake: An uncooked liquid solution of drug(s) that is injected.

cooker: A spoon, bottle cap, etc. used to used to cook drugs.

contract: A special learning experience or sanction for TC clients who violate the rules.

coordinator: The lowest-level salaried staff member in a TC.

cop man: Heroin dealer.

cop money: Money to buy street drugs.

cotton shot, also g-shot: Small dose of drugs used to hold off withdrawal.

crimie: Short for crime partner.

Daytop Village: A drug treatment center, based on a TC model, founded in 1963.

dealer's cut: Heroin before it is cut and marketed for the consumer market.

deuce bag: Two-dollar bag of heroin.

Dilaudid: A morphine derivative known also as drug-store horse/heroin.

drinking privileges: At one time, TCs permitted senior clients to drink, as long as they did so moderately.

drop a slip: TC residents who had "feelings" for another resident or staff member could write their name on a piece of paper and drop it in a special box to ensure they would be placed in the same group.

dyno: Short for dynamite.

encounter groups: Therapy groups in which direct confrontation is emphasized.

expeditor: A TC client who assists the staff in maintaining discipline.

family: Staff and clients at a TC.

Flower Cong: A combination of Flower Child and Viet Cong, often used disparagingly.

fly: Very good, "cool."

general meeting: A special meeting for TC clients, usually called to address a major disciplinary problem.

gimmicks, works: Apparatus for injecting drugs.

guajiros: The country people of Cuba.

guest room: A special room where residents, with staff permission, could have sexual relations.

guilt kills: The belief that clients who don't admit to violating TC rules will eventually end up relapsing.

gut shot: Something said in a group that has a powerful emotional impact.

haircut: A strong verbal reprimand.

hats off: An expression that means that TC residents are permitted to confront staff members in an encounter group.

hoteling it: A TC resident who acts like they are there only because they need a place to stay.

Huey P. Newton: Co-founder of the Black Panther Party for Self-Defense.

hype stick: Apparatus used to inject drugs.

image: A way of projecting oneself that obscures one's inner self.

jackpot: The state of being in trouble.

jíbaro: The country people of Puerto Rico; hick.

learning experience: An administrative sanction, such as a loss of privileges.

lumpen: Underclass.

oil burner: Severe heroin habit.

Panthers/Black Panthers: A revolutionary Black organization founded in California in the '60s.

Papá Dios: God the Father.

pendejo: Fool, jerk (literally, pubic hair).

Phoenix House: New York City's TC system, founded in the 1960s.

playing it safe: Doing as little as possible so as not to attract attention.

P.M.C.: Pennsylvania Military College (1821-1972).

prospect chair: A chair where potential clients for admission into a TC have to wait for an interview.

pull-up: A mild verbal reprimand.

putas estúpidas: Stupid whores.

putting your balls/ovaries on the line: Taking a stand.

reacting: When a TC resident talks back to a staff member.

Red Book: *Quotations from Chairman Mao Tse-tung.*

Red Guard: A militant paramilitary youth organization in China in the 1960s.

Rockefeller Program: A New York State-run residential program for drug addicts.

screw: Prison guard.

speed: Methamphetamine.

speedball: A mixture of heroin and cocaine.

spike: Needle used to inject drugs.

split: To leave a TC without staff authorization.

splitee: A client who leaves a TC on their own.

square: A non-drug user.

Synanon: Founded in 1958, Synanon originally provided residential care for drug addicts, and was "the mother of TCs."

The Prophet: A book of 28 poetic essays by Kahlil Gibran, first published in 1923, that was read with Bible-like reverence in early TCs.

Trane: Nickname for jazz pianist John Coltrane.

trap encounter: Special groups for couples.

yerba (hierba): Marijuana.

Vayas con Dios: Go with God, God be with you.

viejito: An endearing term for an old man.

what goes around comes around: Actions have consequences.

Young Lords: A Puerto Rican revolutionary organization founded in the 1960s.

Discography

"Louie Louie," The Kingsmen

"A Hard Rain's A-Gonna Fall," Bob Dylan

"Uptight (Everything's Alright)," Stevie Wonder

"There but for Fortune," Joan Baez

"Acid," Ray Barretto

"Moody's Mood for Love," King Pleasure

"Everything is Beautiful," Ray Stevens

"Kick Out the Jams," MC5

"What's Your Name," Don and Juan

"Sad Girl," Joe Bataan

"To Be With You," Joe Cuba

"*La Rata*," Joe Cuba

"Long Lonely Nights," Lee Andrew and the Hearts

"Lonely Teardrops," Jackie Wilson

"Tears on My Pillow," Little Anthony and the Imperials

"Billie's Bounce," Charlie "Bird" Parker

"My Favorite Things," John "Trane" Coltrane

"Sittin' On the Dock of the Bay," Otis Redding

"Try a Little Tenderness," Otis Redding

"Pain in My Heart," Otis Redding

"Mr. Pitiful," Otis Redding

"Only the Strong Survive," Jerry Butler

"Raindrops Keep Fallin' on My Head," B.J. Thomas

"Hong Kong Mambo," Tito Puente

"*Torna a Surriento*," Mario Lanza

"*Malafemmena*," Jerry Roselli

Acknowledgements

An earlier version of "Believer," was published in *The New York Times,* April 30, 2006.

"Changing Stripes," *Philadelphia Poets,* Volume 21, pending 2015.

"Just Out of Jail," *Run to the Roundhouse, Nelly,* Winter 2014.

"My Bag, His Bag," *First Literary Review–East,* May, 2012.

"Shooting Dope with Trotsky," *Rutherford Red Wheelbarrow,* Number 3, 2010.

"Kicking in Cuba," *Paterson Literary Review,"* Issue 35, 2006.

An earlier version of "White Uncle Tom," was published in *Fox Chase Review,* Autumn/Winter, 2009.

An earlier version of "Thanksgiving," was published in *Möbius: The Poetry Magazine,* Volume 29, 2011.

"The Meat Rack," "The Queen of Latin Soul," and an earlier version of "Crown of Thorns," were published in *A Blanquito in El Barrio,* Rain Mountain Press, NY, 2009.

"Dopefiend Hustle #132: Playing the Christers," *Shot Glass Journal,* March, 2010.

"Water Games," *Writing Outside the Lines,* (Tammy Nuzzo-Morgan, Peter V. Dugan, eds.), Wild Side Press, NY, 2009.

"Walking Past the Playboy Club, 1971," *Skidrow Penthouse,* Number 17, pending 2015.

An earlier version of "The Battle of Bean Hill," was published in *Bronx Accents*, (Lloyd Ultman and Barbara Unger, eds.), Rutgers University Press, NJ, 2000.

ABOUT THE AUTHOR

Gil Fagiani is an independent scholar, translator, essayist, short story writer, and poet. His translations have appeared in such anthologies as *A New Map: The Poetry of Migrant Writers in Italy*, edited by Mia Lecomte and Luigi Bonaffini; *Poets of the Italian Diaspora*, edited by Luigi Bonaffini and Joseph Perricone; and *Italoamericana: The Literature of the Great Migration, 1880-1943*, edited by Francesco Durante and Robert Viscusi (American Edition).

His first poetry collection *Rooks,* is set at Pennsylvania Military College in the 1960s, (Rain Mountain Press, 2007); *A Blanquito in El Barrio* (Rain Mountain Press, 2009) pulses with the streets and music of Spanish Harlem; *Chianti in Connecticut* (Bordighera Press, 2010) focuses on the immigrant generation of his family, as well as his childhood in Stamford, Connecticut; and *Serfs of Psychiatry* (Finishing Line Press, 2012) was inspired by his experience working in a state psychiatric hospital for twelve years.

Fagiani is a founder and host of the Third Friday, Queens Writers Reading Series in Astoria, New York City, co-curates the Italian American Writers' Association's reading series, and is an associate editor of *Feile-Festa: A Literary Arts Journal*. A social worker and addiction specialist by profession, Fagiani directed a residential treatment program for recovering alcoholics and drug addicts in downtown Brooklyn for 21 years. In 2014, he was the subject of a *New York Times* article by David Gonzalez, "A Poet Mines Memories of Drug Addiction."

OTHER BOOKS BY GIL FAGIANI:

Crossing 116th Street, Skidrow Penthouse (2004)

Rooks, Rain Mountain Press (2007)

Grandpa's Wine, Poets Wear Prada (2008)

A Blanquito in El Barrio, Rain Mountain Press (2009)

Chianti in Connecticut, Bordighera Press (2010)

Serfs of Psychiatry, Finishing Line Press (2012)

Stone Walls, Bordighera Press (2014)

PRAISE FOR PREVIOUS WORK

Stone Walls (Bordighera Books, 2014) administers a dose of Americana with a twist. Gil Fagiani's fifties childhood is recalled with the treats and temptations of post-war prosperity and adolescence rendered in high relief. Beneath the bucolic surface of suburban Connecticut the seeds of a rebellion that will explode a decade later are germinating. These poems are filled with the restlessness of the first generation born after the bomb and portray the initial, impulsive steps toward revolutionary sentiments.

> – Stephen Siciliano, highwayscribery, book reviews

Out of the squishy swamp of dead personal lyrics that is contemporary American poetry, Gil Fagiani's hard-boned zombies rise out of his poetry collection, *A Blanquito in El Barrio* (Rain Mountain Press, 2009). His poems of a white junkie in East Harlem are crafty narratives that sing the music of a lived life: sex, compassion, friendship, justice, mercy, comedy, betrayal, dope and more dope. Fagiani is a poet of unusual power. These poems have strong heart and deep soul ... these are blue collar odes that work. *A Blanquito in El Barrio* is that rare good thing – a necessary good book.

> – Angelo Verga, poet, author of *A Hurricane Is,*
> *33 NYC Poems,* and *Praise For What Remains*

Grandpa's Wine (Poets Wear Prada, 2008) is written where people make a life among the ruins of a shattered world. Feelings and memories take the place of an old coherence, now lost and never to be replaced. Gil Fagiani's poems inhabit this world's poignancy, searching its sorrows with unimpeachable candor and a spare language that perfectly suits its straightforward tastes and its undervalued satisfactions.

– Bob Viscusi, author of *Ellis Island, Astoria: A Novel,* and *An Oration Upon the* Most *Recent Death of Christopher Columbus*

Poets Against the War is like Generals for the War: the poetic imagination and the military strategist are not so much opposite as mutually exclusive. Which is the core reason why Gil Fagiani's *Rooks* is so utterly fascinating – a book of poems that serves as a journal of his first ("rook") year at Pennsylvania Military College. From there, step by step, like a military march to the grave or enlightenment (take your pick – the poet's ambiguity lays it all out, leaving it up to the reader to judge), Fagiani's unblinking observation tells it straight, true, succinct and all poetry. With humor, insight, and a massive dose of humanity, Fagiani charts how boys are hammered into becoming military officers, and in so doing reveals how he himself became a first-rate poet.

– Bob Holman, Proprietor, Bowery Poetry Club